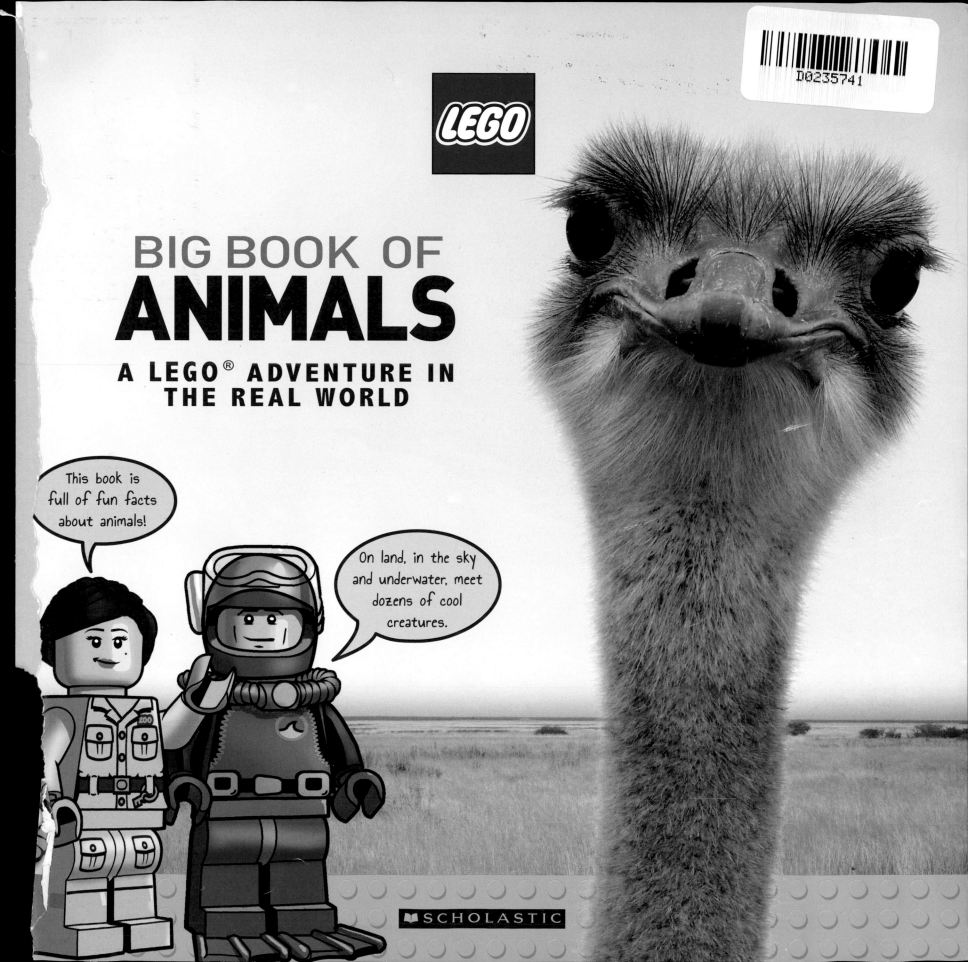

Welcome, LEGO fans!

LEGO® minifigures show you the world in a unique non-fiction series.

This book is part of a series of LEGO non-fiction books with something for all the family, at every age and stage. LEGO non-fiction books have amazing facts, beautiful real-world photos and minifigures everywhere, leading the fun and discovery.

To find out about the books in the series, visit www.scholastic.co.uk

Scholastic Children's Books,
Euston House, 24 Eversholt Street, London NW1 1DB, UK

A division of Scholastic Ltd
London ~ New York ~ Toronto ~ Sydney ~ Auckland
Mexico City ~ New Delhi ~ Hong Kong

This book was first published in the US in 2017 by Scholastic Inc.
Published in the UK by Scholastic Ltd, 2017

ISBN 978 1407 17233 0

Contents

Leaping lizards! I'm looking forward to some snake spotting!

Build it!

Check out the epic building ideas wherever you see me!

No monkeying around, okay? The animals in this book are wild!

Animal adventure

Take a wild ride through the habitats of the world and discover the amazing animals that live in each of them!

Wrap up warm for an Arctic trip! Find out how animals survive on the ice.

Scramble through the hot, steamy rainforest to find colourful animals. Look out! Some animals are well hidden.

Meet the many forest animals who make their homes in and around the trees.

HEAD NORTH for an ice-cold adventure. The Arctic is right at the top of the world. A big part is a frozen ocean, where it's as cold as -40°C (-40°F) in winter. Not many plants grow in the Arctic so finding food in winter is difficult. Animals who live there all year round have developed ways to cope with the extreme conditions.

> I can't wait to chill with a pack of wolves.

> I might have picked the wrong snack...

animals

Polar bear

It's spring in the Arctic. But it's still only around 0°C (32°F). A polar bear mum has thick fur that keeps her toasty and warm. Her cubs are born in a den dug out of snow. When they are big enough, they crawl out onto the Arctic ice.

It's wild!

Polar bears can be as tall as 3.5 m (11 ft 1 in) when stood on their back legs. That's as tall as 87 minifigures!

8

Imagine it! Design an animal that is perfect for the Arctic. What do they need?

> A polar bear looks white, but its skin is black and its fur is see-through.

Minifacts

Type: mammal
Food: seals, small whales, bird's eggs
Sound: growl, chuff
Baby name: cub
Group name: a celebration of polar bears

The cubs stay with their mum for two and a half years, learning how to live on the ice.

> These polar bears are the biggest meat eaters on land in the world. And they can run!

Reindeer

Winter arrives in the Arctic. The reindeers join together in huge groups called herds. They will travel south to find food and warmer weather. Sometimes, half a million join a walk! When groups of animals go on a long journey, it's called a migration. Reindeer migrations are the longest land treks of any animal.

Build it!

Some Arctic people follow the reindeers as they migrate. Build a speedy sledge to whizz them over the ice. Which of your minifigures would enjoy a long, snowy journey?

A reindeer's feet click when it walks. Imagine the racket when a big herd passes by!

Minifacts

Type: mammal
Food: lichens, moss, grass
Sound: bark, whistle
Baby name: calf
Group name: a herd of reindeer

Some reindeers walk 4,328 km (3,000 miles) in one year. That's like snowboarding across the whole of the USA!

Awesome. But can a reindeer fly?

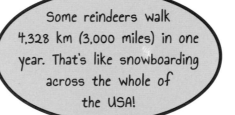

Puffin

What's that flash of red and orange? Puffins gather on the steep cliffs. They spend most of their lives at sea. In the spring, they lay their eggs in burrows. Puffins love to fish in the chilly waters of the Arctic. They swim by flapping their wings as if they are flying.

A puffin's beak is spiky, so it can catch and carry slippery fish. Cool!

● **Play it!** Fisherman follows the puffins out to sea, but his boat has a hole! Help! Who will save him?

In the winter, a puffin's beak turns grey. The show is over!

Minifacts

Type: bird
Food: mainly fish
Sound: purr, grunt, groan
Baby name: puffling
Group name: a circus of puffins

Water mammals

Want to take a chilly dip? Head for the Arctic Ocean! The Arctic is one huge sea surrounded by land. The centre of the Arctic is actually floating ice. In winter the ice is huge, and in summer it starts to melt and get smaller. Some mammals spend all their lives in the ocean. They have bodies that help them to survive in freezing water.

Arggh... this is no way to go ice fishing!

You won't last long in these freezing waters, Explorer. But that's only the tip of the iceberg. Watch out for the bears and whales!

Mammals may head for cold water because it's packed with the tasty sea creatures they like to eat.

Yikes, Ocean King! I could dive into a fish sandwich myself.

Polar bears can swim for a week to find a new ice home.

Beluga whales have a thick layer of fat, called blubber, to keep them warm.

The long-tusked walrus spends some time in water and some time on land.

The orca is a huge dolphin that can hold its breath for 11 minutes!

A baby harp seal pup starts to swim when it is six weeks old.

Wolf

Build it!

Hurry! The wolves are coming! Yeti wants to follow the pack. Build a snowmobile so he can zoom across the ice.

It's quiet in the woods. Suddenly, there's a long, loud howl. The Arctic wolves are nearby. Their white coats are hard to spot in the snow. The wolves hunt together and howl to let each other know where they are. The ground is too frozen to dig a burrow so they live in rocky caves.

Minifacts

Type: mammal
Food: musk ox, reindeers, hares, birds
Sound: howl, bark, whimper, snarl
Baby name: cub
Group name: a pack of wolves

Wolves are always the baddies in stories. Make up a story where wolves are the good guys.

Arctic wolves can be heard from 8 km (5 miles) away. I wonder how loud Wolf Guy can howl?

Arctic animals

Arctic tern

Atlantic puffin

Snow goose

Lemming

Walrus

Arctic fox

Wolverine

Some animals fight the Arctic chill with thick fur or cosy feathers. Others have a layer of blubber to keep them warm. When temperatures drop to their lowest, some snooze through the whole winter. This is called hibernation.

Cod

Ptarmigan

Reindeer

Snowy owl

Harp seal

Harp seal pup

Arctic hare

Polar bear cub

Build it!

Quick! A snowstorm is coming. Ice Fisherman and Snow Boarder need an igloo to shelter in. An igloo is a small, dome-shaped shelter made of hard snow. It is cosy in an Arctic blizzard!

Cosy? Hmmm.

Trust me! Once you're inside an igloo your body heat warms it up. The warm air stays in!

19

IN THE FOREST, tall trees stretch to the sky all around you. Take a walk in the woods and you may have to look hard for the animals! Trees are great to hide up, and many animals have fur that camouflages them against the ground. The forest changes with each season.

You may want to stop talking so loudly! Many woodland animals only come out at night.

Yawn! I'm not much of a night owl...

animals

⬤ Imagine it!

Design and build an animal with colours that keep it hidden in the woods.

Tiger

The biggest cat in the world, the tiger, is on the prowl. It crosses a rushing river to follow its prey. It likes to hunt as the sun goes down. The tiger can see six times better in the dark than we can. Black and orange stripes help it to hide among the branches. The tiger moves silently. Close to its prey now, it suddenly sprints. It runs almost twice as fast as any human. The tiger POUNCES!

Minifacts

Type: mammal
Food: deers and pigs
Sound: roar, chuff, brrr
Baby name: cub
Group name: an ambush of tigers

It eats pigs? I need to save my bacon!

No two tigers have the same pattern of furry stripes. Cool stripes by the way!

It's not just the fur. A tiger's skin is stripy too!

Skunk

Don't upset the striped skunk, it has a cool trick! The sun is going down. The skunk begins a search for food. But there are dangerous animals around. The skunk has short legs and cannot run fast. It has a better way to escape danger. The skunk turns and blasts a stinky mist from under its tail. Phhhewww! That will get rid of any nuisance!

It's wild!

A skunk's stink can be smelt 1.6 km (1 mile) away. I'm keeping my nose out of its business!

Build it!

Skunks live in burrows or shelter in hollow logs. Build a home for a family of stripy skunks to live in.

> Skunks love to munch on honeybees.

Minifacts

Type: mammal
Food: almost anything except butter beans!
Sound: hiss, growl, squeak, coo
Baby name: kitten
Group name: a surfeit of skunks

Spider

It's evening time in the woods. The orb-weaver spider starts to spin a silky web. It makes a brand-new web every day. The spider makes sure some of the strands are sticky, to catch insects as they fly into the web.

Why did the spider buy a computer? She wanted a website!

Play it! Spider Lady and Fly Monster are in the treetops. A shadow appears overhead. What happens?

The spider waits. It hangs upside down on its web, clinging on with eight legs. An insect flies into the sticky web. In seconds, the spider kills it with a bite. It wraps the fly in silk. A tasty snack for later!

The biggest web made by one spider was about 25 m (82 ft) long! Gulp!

Minifacts

Type: arachnid
Food: insects
Sound: none
Baby name: spiderling
Group name: a cluster of spiders

Spiders don't work very hard, they just sit and wait for their food.

Hey, Bumblebee Girl. Who are you calling lazy? It takes the spider about an hour to spin a web.

Woodland animals

Wolf spider

Comma butterfly

Raccoon

The forest trees give shelter from the sun and keep things cool. Trees also provide plenty of food to eat, with berries, leaves, and branches to nibble.

Jay

Woodpecker

Beaver

Adder

Stag beetle

Woodlouse

Peacock butterfly

Goshawk

Wild boar

Red squirrel

Pine marten

Hedgehog

European Toad

Frog

Grass snake

Longhorn beetle

Build it!

Circus Clown and Forest Maiden want to hide in the treetops to watch squirrels and birds. Build them a super-tall tower so they can get a bird's-eye view. Look out for the goshawk!

What do you say to a frog who needs a ride? Hop in!

You're hopping mad, you are...!

29

Owl

The forest is dark. The tawny owl leaves its perch and flies through the trees. Big eyes help it to see, even in the darkness. Its flapping wings make no noise. The owl can hear the tiniest movement on the forest floor. It senses a mouse. In a split second, the owl swoops down to grab its prey.

Build it!

An owl swallows its food whole, then it coughs up a pellet with the bones and fur in it.

We waiters are glad that people don't do that!

Most owls are nocturnal animals. This means they are most active at night. Build a tree with a hollow for an owl to shelter in.

The owl doesn't need to land. It flies straight back up to the skies.

If you make a really good hooting sound in the woods, an owl may hoot back!

Minifacts

Type: bird
Food: small mammals, frogs, birds
Sound: hoot, "kewick" call
Baby name: owlet
Group name: a parliament of owls

Burrowers

Stand in the woods and you can be sure that there is something underneath your feet. Some animals dig underground burrows. They sleep in them, hide from enemies, shelter from the weather and even raise babies. The animals have strong claws to help them dig the earth.

Skunks prefer to steal another animal's burrow, or find somewhere else cosy.

Don't get any ideas about my helmet!

A badger burrow, called a sett, has many tunnels and rooms.

Wood ants make nests that go deep underground.

Porcupines build big burrows, shared between families.

The wolf spider does not spin webs, it digs burrows instead.

A fox sleeps in its underground den during the day.

Bat

What's that clinging upside down to a tree branch with its long claws? It's a bat. Its webbed wings flap down by its side. Bats are the only mammals that fly.

Build it!

Some bats live in caves. Design and build a cave with long tunnels and big rooms for loads of bats to live in.

The bat sleeps all day and hunts at night. It can catch flying insects in total darkness.

The biggest bats have wings that stretch 1.8 m (6 ft) wide! That's batty!

Minifacts

Type: mammal
Food: flying insects, spiders, earwigs
Sound: high-pitched clicks
Baby name: pup
Group name: a colony of bats

A bat can eat up to 1,000 mosquitoes in one hour. That's like a person eating more than their own weight in pizzas!

Woohoo, let's give it a try!

Bats find insects in the dark by clicking and listening for where the echo comes from.

Blindfold me and I'll give it a go.

Click, click, click! This isn't working... Oooof!

Ha, ha, Vampire Bat! That gave me a buzz!

I'm glad I don't hunt that way...

Panda

Deep in the bamboo forests of China lives a very rare bear – the giant panda. The panda is a fussy eater. It mostly eats bamboo, which is super-tough. It has very strong teeth to tear through the shoots. The panda has to chew and chew non-stop for 16 hours a day to fill its tummy! It spends the rest of the day sleeping.

It's wild!

A panda mother is about 900 times bigger than her newborn cub. The cub is only the length of a pencil!

Imagine it!   Imagine you live among the pandas. Design and build a Chinese pagoda.

Minifacts

Type: mammal
Food: bamboo, occasionally other leaves
Sound: squeak, growl, bark, huff
Baby name: cub
Group name: an embarrassment of pandas

BRING AN UMBRELLA if you are going to the rainforest. It rains – a lot. It is also hot. This makes the rainforest the perfect place for plants to grow. And where there are lots of plants, there are always lots of animals. The rainforest has more kinds of animals than almost anywhere else.

The treetops of the forest are called the canopy. Most of the animals live there. You'd better like heights!

Rainforest

animals

Some animals eat plants. Some eat each other! Some plants are pretty dangerous too!

Macaw

It's dawn in the rainforest.
There is a flash of colour
above the trees. Dazzling
scarlet macaws swoop
through the sky. Their
squawks and screeches
echo through the treetops.
They are looking for a
breakfast of fruit
and nuts.

● **Play it!** Lumberjack is climbing a big rainforest tree. He hears voices from up above. Who is there?

A scarlet macaw has a special bone in its tongue that it uses to eat fruit!

Minifacts

Type: bird
Food: fruit, seeds, nuts, flowers, leaves
Sound: screech, squawk, growl
Baby name: chick
Group name: a pandemonium of parrots

A macaw's screech can be heard right across the rainforest, like this horn.

The rainforest is loud enough without you blowing your trumpet!

Oooh, funny hair, funny hair?

Huh? Who said that?

It wasn't me. I didn't say it!

Yeah right. You are so rude!

Go away! Go away!

Ha, ha! Macaws can copy words and lots of other sounds! Watch what you say when there's a parrot around!

Ant

Build it!

Build an enormous robot ant for Jungle Boy to ride on. Add some powerful pincers and long antennae.

Left, right, left, right. An army of 700,000 ants moves through the forest. Nothing is safe in their path. They hunt and eat anything they pass. Run! This army is hungry!

Army ants carry their babies, or larvae, with them as they travel.

Minifacts

Type: insect
Food: other insects, spiders, frogs
Sound: none
Baby name: larva
Group name: an army of ants

Army ants have no nest. When they stop they all cling together, protecting the babies and queen inside.

Nothing more important than a queen! She's the only one that lays the eggs!

Orang-utan

Why go to the forest floor when everything you need is in the treetops? The orang-utan is sitting in her nest. She builds it with leaves and branches. Sometimes, she builds a roof for the nest if it rains too hard. When she is hungry, she will swing from branch to branch to find her favourite food and sip water from leaves.

Orang-utans know when a tree has ripe fruit. They have a "fruit map" of 150 kinds of fruit in their heads!

Remembering that many would drive me bananas!

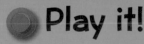 **Play it!** It's pouring

When it rains, orang-utans often make umbrellas out of huge leaves!

Minifacts

Type: mammal
Food: fruit, leaves, bark, ants
Sound: long call, fast call
Baby name: baby
Group name: congress of orang-utans

with rain! Build a nest just like an orang-utan's. Which minifigure will you ask for help?

Camouflage

The rainforest is alive with animal sounds – chirps, squeaks, howls. But sometimes, as hard as you look, you just can't see any animals! They are hidden, or camouflaged, among the leaves and flowers. Some hide so that they won't be eaten. Some are hunters ready to pounce!

I've just dropped in to photograph some critters. So! Where are they?

Sigh. Many are camouflaged. You might want to try blending in too.

This potoo bird blends in with the tree bark!

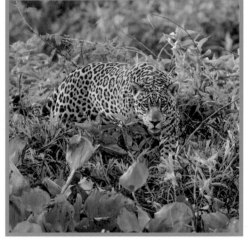

Spots make it difficult to see the jaguar in the undergrowth.

The katydid cricket looks exactly like a leaf!

It's tricky to spot this orchid mantis hiding like a flower!

Any animal hunting this frog would easily miss it!

Frog

There's no need for this frog to be camouflaged. It's one of the most poisonous animals in the world! It is brightly coloured to warn animals not to touch it. Its colours shout "Shoo! Don't eat me!"

Build it!

Fairy-tale Princess is looking for safe frogs to kiss. Build a riverboat that is perfect for frog-spotting along jungle waterways.

The poison is on the frog's skin, so whatever you do, keep away!

Remember. The duller the colour, the more friendly the frog.

Minifacts

Type: amphibian
Food: insects and spiders
Sound: croak
Baby name: tadpole
Group name: a knot of frogs

Can't I give it a little kiss?

Sloth

Take it slow, really slow.
Meet the sloth. It's so slow
that algae grows on its fur,
making it turn green!
Sloths spend all their
lives in the treetops,
hanging out, and
taking it easy!

Build it!

Gorilla Suit Guy
wants to spot
sloths. The
best way is to
travel through
the treetops. Build
a treetop walkway to
connect all the trees in
your rainforest.

Moths, beetles and cockroaches like to live in a sloth's fur.

Minifacts

Type: mammal
Food: leaves, twigs, shoots
Sound: squeaks and eeks
Baby name: baby
Group name: they tend to live alone

Sloths have very long claws that grip branches tightly while they eat... slowly!

It's wild!

A sloth only ever visits the ground to go to the toilet. It's a day trip to get there and it only goes once a week!

Rainforest animals

Toucan

Malachite Kingfisher

Parrot

Jaguar

Check out the rainforest rainbow! Not all animals are camouflaged, some are super-bright! But be careful, the colourful ones are often poisonous!

Gorilla

Rainbow boa

Gibbon

Lantern moth

Pygmy marmoset

Armadillo

Jewel beetle

Strawberry poison dart frog

Amazonian bush cricket

Leafcutter ant

Daggerwing butterfly

Fruit bat

Green tree python

Blue morpho

Capybara

Giant centipede

Tarantula

Build it!

Zoo Keeper wants a treehouse that reaches the top of the trees. Build the tallest one you can. Remember to add a balcony for watching the animals!

The Korowai people in South East Asia build treehouses that reach all the way to the top of the rainforest trees.

Gulp! That's high!

53

Butterfly

The forest floor is dark. A large morpho butterfly sits with its wings shut together. It is camouflaged against the ground. The butterfly is startled. It opens its wings to fly away and FLASH! Its wings are bright blue inside!

It's wild!

The morpho butterfly is one of the biggest butterflies in the world. It's almost as big as a page in this book!

● **Play it!** Pilot is watching the morphos from his plane.

The beautiful blue inside its wings sparkles through the trees as the butterfly flies up to the sky.

The wings are covered in tiny scales that shine blue in the light. Dazzling!

Minifacts

Type: insect
Food: nectar from flowers
Sound: none
Baby name: caterpillar
Group name: a rabble of butterflies

Tally-ho! Pilots in small planes can sometimes spot the flashing blue of the morphos as they fly over the rainforest.

Ping! I flash blue too. Back in a flash!

A storm arrives. Where will he land?

Python

The green tree python is green but its babies aren't! The babies are born yellow, brown or even red! Often they have spots or stripes too. The babies turn green as they grow up.

It's wild!

The green tree python only needs to eat four or five times a year!

Play it! Snake Charmer and Explorer have discovered a ruined temple deep in the jungle. They hear a

Boas swallow their prey whole - eww!

Minifacts

Type: reptile
Food: small mammals and reptiles
Sound: hiss
Baby name: hatchling
Group name: a knot of snakes

noise coming from a hole in the wall. What happens next?

Chameleon

The chameleon sits completely still on a branch. Its eyes focus in on a tasty insect. In a split second, it shoots out its super-long, sticky tongue... and ZAP!

Build it!

Chameleons can change colour depending on the mood they are in. How are you feeling, Genie?

Genie loves all the different colours in the jungle. Build a multicoloured lizard. How does it catch its prey? Is it poisonous?

A chameleon's tongue is twice as long as its body. Give me a buzz when it's gone!

It's wild!

The chameleon can move its eyes in different directions. It can look at two things at once!

Minifacts

Type: reptile
Food: insects
Sound: huff
Baby name: baby chameleon
Group name: a lounge of lizards

The tongue is snapped back and the insect is history.

Hmm, I'm feeling a bit blue today.

It's going to be a tough mountain to climb! Grab your gear and I'll show you the ropes!

Mountain

MOUNTAINS are pretty tough places to live! They are sometimes cold, snowy and very, very windy. The higher up an animal lives the less food there is. They have to be excellent at climbing steep slopes and rocky ridges... with no ropes!

Some people think that the yeti – a huge, hairy man monster – lives in the Himalayas in Asia.

I certainly haven't seen one...

animals

Snow Leopard

It's quiet up in the snowy mountains. There seems to be nothing around. But there are eyes watching.

1, 2, 3, LEAP! When snow leopards leap and land they balance perfectly. Just like me!

Hmmm, that might not work for you on a rocky mountain...

Build it!

Oh no! Clumsy Guy wants to climb the mountain AGAIN. Quick! Build a mountain rescue plane. Who knows what scrapes he'll get into this time?

The powerful snow leopard hunts by itself. Its spotty fur blends with the mountains. Its extra-large paws act like snowshoes as it prowls.

Snow leopards wrap their long tails around themselves to keep warm! Cosy!

Minifacts

Type: mammal
Food: wild sheep and goats, ibex, tahrs
Sound: hiss, chuff, mew, growl, wail
Baby name: cub
Group name: they live on their own

Eagle

It's wild!

A golden eagle's talons are thought to be 10 times stronger than a human hand. Handy!

● **Imagine it!**   Skydiver wants to make some wings to help him soar. But where will he fly to?

● Minifacts

Type: bird
Food: small mammals, rodents, birds, fish
Sound: high yelp: Kee-yep
Baby name: eaglet
Group name: a convocation of eagles

High above the mountains, the golden eagle glides through the air. Its huge wings are spread wide. It hardly flaps them. It can stay in the air for hours. The eagle's eyes zoom in on the ground below. It can spot a rabbit from 3.2 km (2 miles) up. Even as it dives down, it keeps its eagle eyes on the rabbit.

Mountain animals

Monarch butterflies

Animals that live in the mountains are not often brightly coloured. Most are brown or grey to blend in with the rocks and earth. Some even turn white in snowy months to keep themselves hidden.

Ibex

Gorilla

Snow leopard

Marmot

Brown hare

Snow finch

Pika

Bearded vulture

Alpine chough

Swift

Andean condor

Himalayan pheasant

Build it!

Rapper does not want to climb a mountain. But he wants to spot the animals. Build a super-cool aeroplane to cruise around in. Give Rapper a bird's-eye view!

What is my favourite dance style? Hip Hop!

Ha, ha! Hares can leap four times higher than their own height. High-five, man!

Brown bear

Autumn arrives in the mountains. The brown bear
knows that it will be difficult to find food in the winter.
It eats and eats until it is really big. The bear
then settles down for a long winter nap.
It won't wake up until the spring.
Goodnight bear!

Build it!

Remember Hot Dog Guy,
when bears are eating for winter,
they can eat up to a quarter
of their body weight
in a day!

Help! I
hope bears don't
like mustard!

Hot Dog Guy is
stuck up the
mountain!
There's a storm
brewing and a
bear is headed straight
for him! Build a 4x4
vehicle that can climb
up mountain tracks.

A bear's claws can be as long as your hand!

Minifacts

Type: mammal
Food: plants, small mammals, fish
Sound: huff, growl, chomp, bark
Baby name: cub
Group name: a sloth of bears

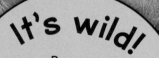

It's wild!

Brown bears may be large, but they are speedy. They can run at up to 48 kph (30 mph)!

Mountain climbers

The one thing animals have to do well if they live on a mountain is climb. And no animals do that better than the the goat and sheep family. They have special feet that deal with steep cliffs and loose rocks... and great balance!

Okay, let's see how much of a Daredevil you are. Let's follow that goat!

Are you kidding me? How does it do that?

Get a grip! A mountain goat's hooves are made for climbing. Its feet grip like climbing shoes.

Will Daredevil make it? It's a bit of a cliffhanger!

You can count the number of rings on a mountain goat's horns to find out how old it is!

I'm glad I'm not a goat! You're not getting near my horns!

The Rocky Mountain goat has a thick coat to keep it warm.

The tahr lives on Everest, Earth's highest mountain.

The Barbary sheep is the only wild sheep living in Africa.

Ibex have been seen climbing walls built by people!

Bighorn sheep can perch on the steepest mountainsides!

Yak

A mountain is the only place for a yak. The huge cow cousin has super-thick hair to keep it warm. Its fur sometimes touches the ground, like a hairy skirt. In winter, snow builds up on its back but it STILL doesn't get cold!

It's wild!

Baby yaks, or calves, get up to walk when they are 10 minutes old. They have to get away from the snow leopards.

Play it!

Computer Programmer is following a yak. Suddenly he hears a roar. What happens next?

Mountain people make cosy sweaters out of yak wool.

Minifacts

Type: mammal
Food: grass, herbs, lichens, moss
Sound: grunt, snort
Baby name: calf
Group name: a herd of yaks

Even I wouldn't wrestle a yak. They are super-tough. Nobody wants a yak whack!

Come on, come on! We need to find the yaks! Hurry up!

Okay, okay. Huff, puff, I'm trying...

Mountain people milk yaks and turn their milk into butter tea. Oops, it's a cow!

Keep going! Left, right, left, right. Up we go!

If you'd just stop yaking...

Desert

Phew! It's hot in the desert! There is little or no rain so plants can't grow easily. Drinking water is difficult to find. The ground may be covered in sand or dry rock. Desert animals have some very clever ways to survive. From tails that shade to big ears that cool, find out how these creatures beat the heat.

We're having a bit of a hot spell, aren't we?

Some deserts are hot in the summer and extremely cold during the winter.

animals

Camel

A sandstorm is coming.
But the camel will be okay!
It closes its nostrils and lips
so that sand cannot get in.
Its wide hooves let it cross
the sand without sinking.

It's wild!

If a camel
is thirsty, it
could drink a full
bath of water in
10 minutes!

Play it! Explorer sees

a minifigure on a

Minifacts

Camels have two rows of eyelashes to keep sand out. Achoo!

Type: mammal
Food: plants - even thorny ones!
Sound: growl, gurgle, hum
Baby name: calf
Group name: a herd of camels

A camel's hump is like a storage jar. It is filled with fat. When there is no food around the camel's body uses its hump fat to keep it going!

Asian camels have two humps, while Arabian ones have just one. One lump or two?

camel in the distance. Who is it? A friend?

Scorpion

The afternoon is the hottest time of day in the desert. A scorpion shelters in a burrow. But at night it scuttles out and goes on the hunt.

Build it!

The Knight wants to escape the scuttling scorpions! Build a desert castle with high walls and tall towers to keep the crazy critters away!

Scorpions have eight legs and are related to spiders. But they still eat them. Ugh!

Minifacts

Type: arachnid
Food: insects, lizards, snakes, rodents
Sound: none
Baby name: baby scorpion
Group name: a nest of scorpions

The sting on its tail is held high over its back. It is looking for a juicy bug to catch. When it finds a bug, the tail curves forward in a split second, stinging its prey. Lunch!

I'm copying the scorpion! It has a hard shell, like armour, that protects it from the strong sun and sandy winds.

Some scorpions glow under a special light. You just need this torch.

Woahhh! They are everywhere! Why do they glow?

No one knows. Perhaps they are glowing with happiness!

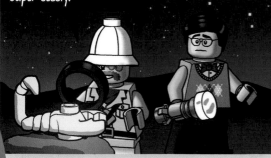

The ones with smaller claws have a worse sting in the tail. This critter is super-deadly!

Yikes, enough info! I think I preferred being left in the dark!

Desert reptiles

Reptiles love hot places. They warm their bodies up in the hot sun. But the desert can get too hot, and there is very little water around. Desert reptiles have some incredible ways to survive.

What are you doing? That looks like hot work!

I'm digging a hole. Some desert reptiles stay in underground burrows to keep cool during the day.

Are you telling me I could be standing on top of a reptile? Snakes alive!

Yes, some snakes bury themselves in sand to keep cool. Keep digging! This snake is ssssizzling!

I say, chaps, the desert gets REALLY cold at night.

I'm shivering even in this sweater! How long until the sun comes back?

The desert tortoise can last a year without drinking water.

This gecko licks the morning dew off its eyeballs to drink.

Water drops roll off the back of this thorny devil into its mouth.

The lizard stands on two feet at a time to keep its other feet cool.

The sidewinder moves over the hot sand in an 's' shape.

Meerkat

A mob of meerkats has left its underground burrow to find food. The meerkats warm themselves up in the sun while one stands guard. It finds the highest piece of ground in the area. It stands tall keeping a watch for danger. Suddenly, a bird of prey hovers overhead. The guard whistles. The meerkats know they are in danger and scurry underground.

Build it!

Meerkats move very fast. They give Royal Guard an idea. Build a desert rally car for him with huge wheels to race across the sand.

A meerkat can look directly at the sun without shades... smooth!

Minifacts

Type: mammal
Food: beetles, scorpions, lizards, spiders
Sound: chirrs, whistles, barks
Baby name: pup
Group name: a mob of meerkats

It's wild!

Meerkats will eat a scorpion. First, they bite off its sting. That way it can't hurt them. Clever!

Desert animals

Some desert animals have bodies that help them cool down. Many animals are pale in colour to help keep them cool and hidden in the sand.

Scarab beetle

Darkling beetle

Sinai agama

Thorny devil

Jerboa

Sandgrouse

Dingo

Addax antelope

Gila monster

Cape ground squirrel

Desert scorpion

84

Horned viper

Spider beetle

Desert monitor

Roadrunner

Bearded dragon

Meerkat

Desert tortoise

Legless lizard

Fennec fox

Build it!

An oasis is a small, green area in the desert. Plants grow around a spring or lake. An oasis is a great place to camp as animals visit to drink. Build an oasis with a hideout near the water to watch the animals.

How do tortoises talk to each other? By shellphone!

Funny! But just keep away from lizard jokes...

Rattlesnake

There is a rattling sound somewhere on the sand. The rattle gets louder. Suddenly, a head shoots up and hisses loudly. The diamond rattlesnake is yelling, "Keep away!" It's enough to make anything run... FAST! The snake shakes its tail to make the rattle. It's a warning that it has a deadly bite.

It's wild!

The tail's end is made of pieces of hard keratin. That's the same material as your nails. The keratin pieces rattle against each other.

Snakes alive! Let's not get rattled.

ER60082

● Play it! Which of your minifigures

This snake can rattle 50 times a second. Much faster than me!

Minifacts

Type: reptile
Food: small rodents and lizards
Sound: hiss, rattle
Baby name: snakelet
Group name: a rhumba of rattlesnakes

could live in the desert?

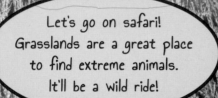

Let's go on safari! Grasslands are a great place to find extreme animals. It'll be a wild ride!

Grassland

GRASSLANDS are areas where there is not enough rain to grow a forest, but there is too much rain for it to be a desert. The main plants are – you guessed it – grasses! Many of the biggest, tallest, most impressive animals in the world live on grasslands, as well as some of the biggest herds.

Ahhh, grasslands sound perfect. I'd love to hop there.

It's actually packed with predators. You'd better hop quickly!

animals

Giraffe

A giraffe has the best view of the grasslands. With its super-long neck, it's the tallest animal in the world. But it still has the same amount of neck bones as you and me. A giraffe's tongue is as long as your arm so it can reach super-high and up into the acacia tree!

It's wild!

Giraffes only sleep for about half an hour a day – and they almost always sleep standing up!

◯ **Play it!** Help Explorer build a ladder to reach as high as the giraffes! How high can you go?

A giraffe's legs are taller than an adult human.

Minifacts

Type: mammal
Food: acacia leaves and other plants
Sound: quiet snorts, whistles, hums
Baby name: calf
Group name: a tower of giraffes

A giraffe's tongue and lips are super-tough to avoid the prickly thorns of the acacia tree! Ouch!

Zebra

Stripes, stripes everywhere! 700,000 zebra gather together to begin a long journey across Africa. They travel every year to find food and water. This horse relative must be careful. There are crocodiles lurking in the river and lions waiting to pounce!

What did the zebra say when it had a sore throat? I'm a little hoarse!

Play it! If anyone can find out where the

Minifacts

Every zebra has its very own stripes. No two zebras look the same.

Type: mammal

Food: grass, herbs, leaves, twigs

Sound: bray (like a donkey)

Baby name: foal

Group name: a dazzle of zebras

zebras are heading, it's Detective! What vehicle should he take?

Lion

A lion rests in the grass. He lives with his family, or pride. He can relax. There is very little danger to lions on the grasslands. But the lion watches for other male lions who might take his hunting ground.
He roars.

Build it!

The King and Queen are going on safari. They want to build a castle so they can watch the animals. Build a castle with an awesome viewing platform.

His roar can be heard from 8 km (5 miles) away. Nothing is going to mess with the king of the animals!

Male lions may sleep up to 20 hours a day. Nice!

Minifacts

Type: mammal
Food: animals such as wildebeests and impalas
Sound: roar, grunt, snarl, growl
Baby name: cub
Group name: a pride of lions

I'm the king and I demand my dinner!

No chance! Female lions may do all the hunting but that doesn't apply to you, lazybones!

Amazing animal builders

Okay, team challenge. Some termites build mounds up to 9 m (30 ft) high. No machines.

Many animals build awesome homes. Some build nests, some dig burrows. It's dangerous out on the grasslands. These super-builders build crazy homes to stay safe!

You want us to build without a digger? Who are you kidding?

Termites position the mound so that the sun doesn't make it too hot.

They also farm a fungus inside that makes food for them...

Okay, stop bugging me! So you want air conditioning and a garden, built by hand... These are crazy critters!

The biggest wasp nest ever found was as big as a car!

The massive weaver bird nest is home to up to 400 birds!

Most wasps chew wood into paper to make a nest.

Tiny termites may build huge towers twice as tall as a person!

Imagine getting caught in that web. Uggghh!

Two hamerkop birds build HUGE nests, some using 10,000 twigs!

Some spiders work together to build gigantic, strong webs!

It's wild!

One dung beetle can drag 1,000 times its own weight – that's like a human pulling six double-decker buses!

Dung beetle

A pile of elephant dung has appeared on the ground. Stinky! But along come the cleaners. The dung beetle pats the poop into a ball and rolls it away. The beetle buries it, then lays its egg in the ball. When the babies are born, they gobble it up.

Play it! The Pharaoh wants to build a pyramid. What could you hide inside it?

The Ancient Egyptians believed that a dung beetle god, Khepri, rolled the sun across the sky each day.

Minifacts

Type: insect
Food: dung
Sound: wings that whirr or buzz
Baby name: larva
Group name: none

Dung beetle fossils show that beetles cleared up dino poop, too.

These beetles have been cleaning up for millions of years. That's cool!

Springbok

A huge herd of antelopes, called springboks, is grazing on the open grasslands. There is a sudden movement. Danger is near and there is nowhere to hide. One springbok leaps high into the air, twice its own height! The leap, known as pronking, warns the others and gives the springbok a good view of the danger. The herd sees and races away at 88 kph (55 mph) to safety.

Build it!

Ballerina is leaping around with the springboks. Build some hurdles for her to leap over. How high can she leap?

A springbok can survive for months without drinking. I'd miss my tea!

Minifacts

Type: mammal
Food: grass and other plants
Sound: grunt, cry
Baby name: calf
Group name: a herd of springboks

Watch me pronk like a springbok!

Hmmm, pronking means "showing off" in the Afrikaans language!

Grassland animals

The grasslands of the world are home to so many different animals. From the fastest animal, the cheetah, and the biggest bird, the ostrich, to the woolly alpacas and giant bison.

Vulture

Termite

Bee-eater

Bison

Ratel

Cheetah

Paper wasp

Secretary bird

Agama

Hyena

Termite

Buffalo

Hippopotamus

African rock python

Rhinoceros

Round-eared elephant shrew

Lilac-breasted roller

Dung beetle

Black mamba

Weaver bird

Warthog

Alpaca

Gerenuk

Rhea

Build it!

Animal Controller is looking forward to taking the minifigures out in a safari jeep. Build one for your adventurers with open sides. No clowning around, these animals are big!

How did the lion stop his TV show? He pressed his paws button! Ha, ha!

Hmm, I wish I could pause all your jokes!

An elephant's skin is so sensitive, it can feel a fly landing on it!

Minifacts

Type: mammal
Food: roots, grasses and other plants
Sound: trumpet, low rumbles
Baby name: calf
Group name: a herd of elephants

Elephant

Out of the way! The biggest animals in the world are coming through. A herd of elephants moves over the grasslands. They live in a close family group and travel to find water. Elephants have excellent memories and can find watering holes they visited years before. They can smell water from many miles away with their amazing trunks.

Play it! Can you remember all your minifigures without looking?

Kangaroo

In the grasslands and woodlands of Australia, kangaroos hop by. What's that on the kangaroo's tummy? It's a baby, called a joey. Kangaroo mums have a pouch like a pocket that their babies grow in.

Build it!

Boxer wants to find boxing kangaroos! Build him a pickup truck so he can cruise the grasslands. Which of your minifigures will he take?

It's wild!

Kangaroos can jump over one another and hop as fast as racehorses.

Animals that have pouches are called marsupials.

Minifacts

Type: mammal
Food: grass, leaves and roots
Sound: grunt, cough, hiss
Baby name: joey
Group name: a mob of kangaroos

Male kangaroos box each other when they are hopping mad! Find me a kangaroo!

No problem, mate. There are more kangaroos than humans in Australia.

DIVE IN and discover life in the water! Whether it's a river, a lake or a huge ocean, there are all kinds of animals swimming, snacking and even sleeping in water. See eight-legged octopuses, hungry hippos and watch out for the sharks!

Over a million different kinds of creatures live in water. Let's explore the watery world.

Water

animals

Penguin

Some penguins spend nine months of the year at sea. Nobody knows how they sleep. Perhaps they take short naps at the surface?

SPLASH! The emperor penguins dive in. These huge birds can't fly through the air but they zip through the water at top speed. Emperor penguins live right at the bottom of the world in the chilly waters near Antarctica. The penguins spend most of their lives at sea.

Play it! Which of your minifigures would enjoy the Antarctic?

Once a year, the penguins return to land. The females lay one egg each. The fluffy chicks are born in the spring.

Emperor penguins are about the size of a 6-year-old human.

Minifacts

Type: bird
Food: fish, crustaceans, squid
Sound: squawks, whistles
Baby name: chick
Group name: a parcel of penguins

Cool! Snoozing not sinking!

Shark

The ocean is calm. All of a sudden there is a CRASH! A shark bursts up through the water. It bares a mouthful of dagger-sharp teeth. Meet the fiercest and largest predator fish – the great white shark. Great whites can be half the length of a bus and swim at up to 60 kph (37 mph).

Fins help a shark to steer and move. I'm going to make a move now!

It's wild!

A great white shark can smell a drop of blood from 3 km (1.8 miles) away.

● **Play it!** Diver and Deep-sea diver are looking for a sunken treasure chest. They find it, but a shark has got

This shark has 300 teeth. That's jawsome!

Minifacts

Type: fish
Food: seals, fish, turtles
Sound: none
Baby name: pup
Group name: a shiver of sharks

Did you know some sharks live 1,500 m (5,000 ft) down in the ocean? That's a deep subject.

I'm going to follow that huge shark to see where it stops. Coming?

No thanks... Tee-hee! You may be gone for a while.

Wow, it's been hours. When will this big fish stop? I need to catch my breath.

Ha, ha! Most sharks need to keep moving to breathe. It will never, ever stop!

there first. What happens next?

Ocean danger

Don't be fooled by how pretty some ocean creatures look. Their amazing shapes and colours may be letting you know that they are very dangerous. Venom is a poison that is injected by biting or stinging. Many sea creatures use venom to protect themselves from predators.

Whoa! All these creatures are so colourful!

Hmmm, there's something fishy about that octopus. Yikes! It's coming for us!

Keep away from that octopus! Some are fully armed – with venom.

Sigh... Those divers never learn. They always find themselves in deep water!

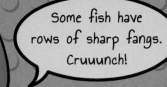

Some fish have rows of sharp fangs. Cruuunch!

Yikes! Munchers and crunchers or super-stingers! I don't know which is worse!

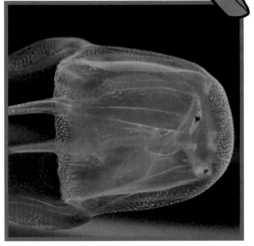

The box jellyfish is one of the most deadly stinging animals.

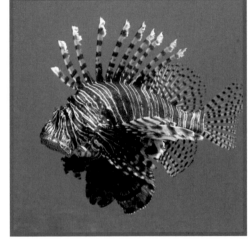

Some of the lionfish's spines can deliver a nasty sting.

The sea krait is ten times more venomous than a rattlesnake!

The blue-ringed octopus' rings flash a warning to keep away.

The cone shell can kill a fish in a single second.

Crocodile

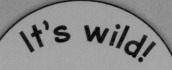

It's wild!
The saltwater croc has the strongest bite of any animal in the world. That's one massive crunch!

Crocodiles lurk, very still, in lakes and rivers where it's hot and steamy. The saltwater croc is the most

Build it!

Sound the alarm! Explorer has found himself in croc-infested waters. Hurry! Build a powerful boat so that Lifeguard can rescue him. Will he escape those snapping jaws?

Minifacts

Type: reptile
Food: fish, birds, mammals
Sound: hiss, bellow, chirp
Baby name: hatchling
Group name: a congregation of crocodiles

massive on Earth. It can be 7 m (23 ft) long. When the croc is hungry, it floats near the shore. With a sudden thrash of its tail, the croc explodes through the water and SNAP! Its huge jaws crunch down.

Turtle

The turtle is looking for its favourite snack. It swims through the water flapping its flippers. It is hunting for jellyfish, its favourite food. The turtle has to breathe air at the surface of the sea. But it can hold its breath for two hours while it hunts under water! Its hard shell protects it from predators as it swims.

It's wild!

One type of turtle travelled all the way across the Pacific Ocean, just to find jellies. It took a year!

● Imagine it!

Design a colourful new jellyfish.

Turtles sometimes cry. But they aren't sad. They cry to get rid of salt from their bodies.

Turtles lived on Earth with the dinosaurs!

Minifacts

Type: reptile
Food: jellyfish, sea sponges, crabs
Sound: honk
Baby name: hatchling
Group name: a turn of turtles

The turtle spends all its life in the sea and only lands on a beach to lay its eggs.

Octopus

Ocean animals

Some of the most beautiful and strangest animals of all live in the ocean. There are millions more kinds yet to be discovered.

Sardines

Hammerhead shark

Squid

Cuttlefish

Sea urchin

Starfish

Cowfish

Pipefish

Conger eel

Porcupine fish

Yellowfin tuna

Eagle ray

Stingray

Seahorse

Jellyfish

Sea anenome and clownfish

Butterfly fish

Build it!

Diver wants to dive down REALLY deep. He will need a deep-sea submersible. Build a sub, and design it for two, so that Diver and Hollywood Starlet can go on an adventure.

Which fish is the most famous? The starfish!

Hmmm, all the fish are stars to me!

Flamingo

A pink flamingo stamps in the shallow lake water. It stirs up the mud with its webbed feet and reaches down with its long neck.

Flamingos eat upside down AND under water. Oh, and they often stand on one leg too. You try it.

Build it!

Popstar wants to watch the pink flamingos. Design and build a lake island fit for a pop princess.

Flamingos are born white. They turn pink as they grow up because of the food they eat!

Flamingos snack on shrimp and algae. I want to be pink, pass the platter please...

Minifacts

Type: bird
Food: brine shrimp, algae
Sound: honk, grunt, growl
Baby name: chick
Group name: a flamboyance of flamingos

I'm not sure that's a good idea for me.

Hippopotamus

Hippos love being in the water. They spend more than half the day floating in water to keep their big bodies cool under the hot sun.

Build it!

Hippos may look a bit chubby, but they can run faster than a human!

Surfer has got too close to the hippo. Hippos are dangerous. Quick! Build a bridge over the water so that Surfer can jump out of the way!

Hippos can weigh 4,500 kg (4.5 tons). Imagine picking that up! Like a small truck!

Minifacts

Type: mammal
Food: grass
Sound: snort, grumble, honk, whine
Baby name: calf
Group name: a bloat of hippos

Yikes! Thank goodness they can't jump!

When they want to move, they close their nostrils and ears. The heavy hippos sink to the bottom of the lake. They can walk right along the lake bed, holding their breath for up to five minutes before popping up again. When it's cooler, they leave the water to nibble on grass.

Glossary

Amphibian
A cold-blooded vertebrate that is born in water and breathes with gills. Frogs and toads are amphibians.

Arachnid
An invertebrate with eight legs and two body sections. Spiders and scorpions are arachnids.

Blubber
The layer of fat under the skin of a sea mammal that helps keep it warm.

Burrow
A hole, tunnel or series of chambers dug by a small animal to live in.

Camouflage
Natural colouring that helps animals blend in with their surroundings.

Canopy
The highest branches of the trees in a rainforest, making a spreading layer.

Den
A wild animal's hidden home.

Habitat
The natural home or environment of an animal, plant or other living thing.

Herd
A group of animals that live or travel together.

Hibernation
Spending the winter sleeping or resting.

Hooves
The covering protecting the foot of certain animals. Hooves is the plural of hoof.

Insect
A land invertebrate with three body sections, six legs and often two pairs of wings.

Larva
An animal in the second stage of its life, after it hatches from an egg and before it is an adult. The plural of larva is larvae.

Mammal
A warm-blooded animal that has hair and breathes air.

Female mammals produce milk to feed their young.

Migrate
To move from one place to another to find food, to have babies or to escape from cold weather.

Nocturnal
An animal that is most active at night. Many animals, such as owls and bats, are nocturnal.

Predator
An animal that hunts and eats other animals.

Prey
An animal that is hunted and eaten by another animal.

Reptile
A cold-blooded animal with scaly skin that lays eggs. Snakes and crocodiles are reptiles.

You were right. Those animals are wild, really wild!

Index

Why don't monkeys play cards in the grasslands? There are too many cheetahs!

Thanks

For Scholastic UK: Penny Arlon and Tory Gordon-Harris

For the LEGO® Group: Peter Moorby, Licensing Coordinator ; Heidi K. Jensen, Licensing Manager ; Paul Hansford, Creative Publishing Manager ; Martin Leighton Lindhardt, Publishing Graphic Designer ; Tara Wike, Design Manager ; Anette Dall, Associate Marketing Manager.

Picture credits